Morning Work for Teens With Special Needs Workbook
(August, September, October & November)

© 2024 by S. B. Linton. www.autismclassroom.com

All rights reserved.

This book may not be stored in a retrieval system, or transmitted by any means electronic, mechanical, recording, or otherwise, without written permission from the author. Photocopying for use in the classroom is allowed.

Morning Work for Teens With Special Needs Workbook (August, September, October & November)

What's Included...	Page
Introduction	3
August	5
September	55
October	101
November	151

Introduction...

This workbook is designed for students with significant challenges. It spans four months (August, September, October and November) covering back to school and fall-themed topics. It is designed for 6th through 12th grade students with intellectual disabilities. The packet features age-appropriate worksheets where possible. It includes a variety of response styles such as circling, cutting and pasting, marking and pointing. While the activities are designed for a short morning work activity, students may still require supervision and support to complete them.   -Enjoy!

August

Morning Work for Teens with Special Needs

For 6th – 12th grade students with significant special needs.

Morning Work for Teens
Name: _____

7

August

Summer Camp Post Card

Directions: Color a note for a family member. Cut it out and deliver it to them.

The summer can be fun.

It is important to stay safe near the water.

SPLASH

I am having fun in the sun!

Let's chill together!

From:

Morning Work for Teens   q   August

Name:

Beach
Word Search

Directions: The word beach appears several times below. Dot, highlight or circle the word beach.

swim
            20   beach   10
   31   23
                                        25
beach   17   3
    2
                 hot   beach
   30   5   9
      beach
                           11
   4   7   14
              sun   beach

   31   sand   3
                         6   2

Morning Work for Teens
Name:_____

11

August

Beach Day Fun

Can you locate the same pictures and mark them?

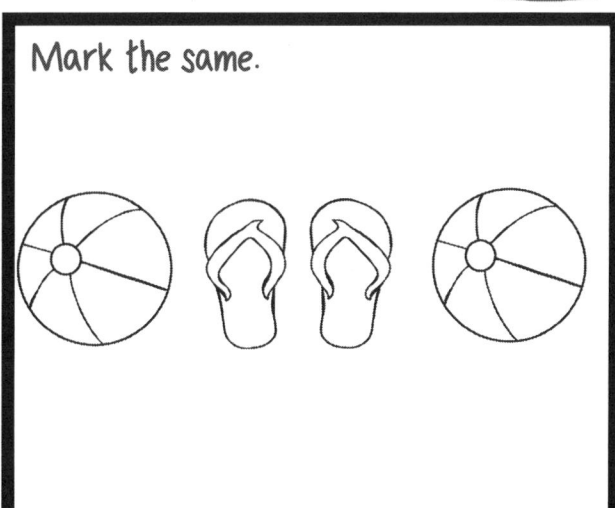

SUN SPF50

Mark the same.

Mark the same.

Mark the same.

Mark the same.

Morning Work for Teens

Name: _____

13

August

Back to School

Directions: Draw a line to tell which items you may see in the classroom.

I might see paper.

I might see a scissors.

I might see books.

I might see glue.

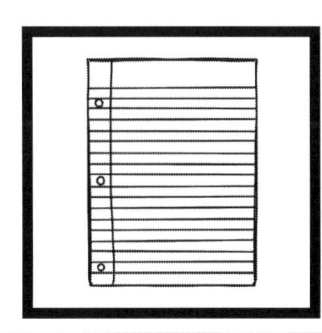

Morning Work for Teens

15 August

Name: _____

Fun in the Sun

Fill in the Letters

Directions: Fill in the correct letters to finish the words to say Happy Mother's Day.

f _ n

_ n   t _ e

s u _

| u | i | n | h |

Morning Work for Teens

Name:

17

August

Find the word

Directions: Use a marker or colored pencil to color in any box that spells summer correctly.

	musmer	
summer	emblem	mlembs
sremu	summer	surem
summer	sumre	summer
mums	sums	summer
summer	summer	mummes

Morning Work for Teens

Name:

19

August

National Summer Sun Safety Month

Directions:
1. Cut and match to the same picture.
2. Color in the two pictures.
3. Circle the word sun.

sun

| sun | mus | sun | sand | sun | tun | pin | sun |
| say | sun | spy | sty | sky | sun | run | sun |

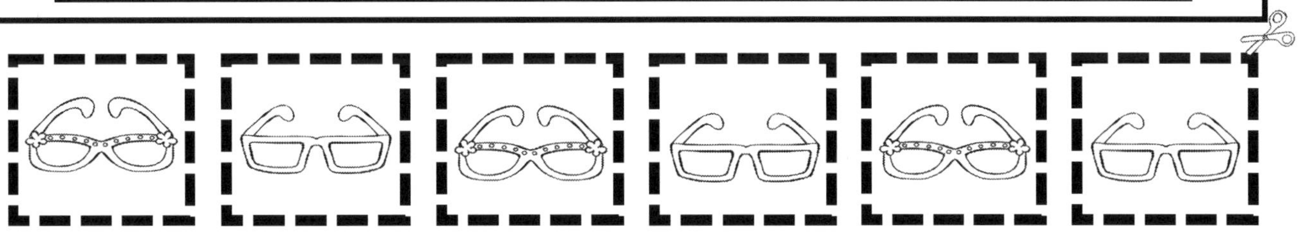

Morning Work for Teens

Name:

21

August

Actions Match

Directions:
1. Use pencil, string or thread to connect the pictures that match.
2. Cut and paste the correct word to the picture.

Who is sleeping?

Who is winking?

Who is smiling?

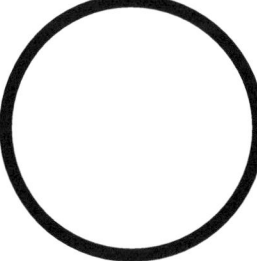

winking

smiling

sleeping

Morning Work for Teens

Name: _____

23

August

Word Search

Directions: Circle the words.

August

| cool | happy | August | sick | August |
| August | where | what | August | tooth |

school

school   send   stop   school   sun   school   cycle   school
son   scent   school   schooling   school   scissors   school

students

students   stop   students   stopping   sitting
seconds   students   stun   sun   students

Morning Work for Teens

Name:

25

August

August
Bingo Marker Fun

Directions: Dot or mark the words the correct color.

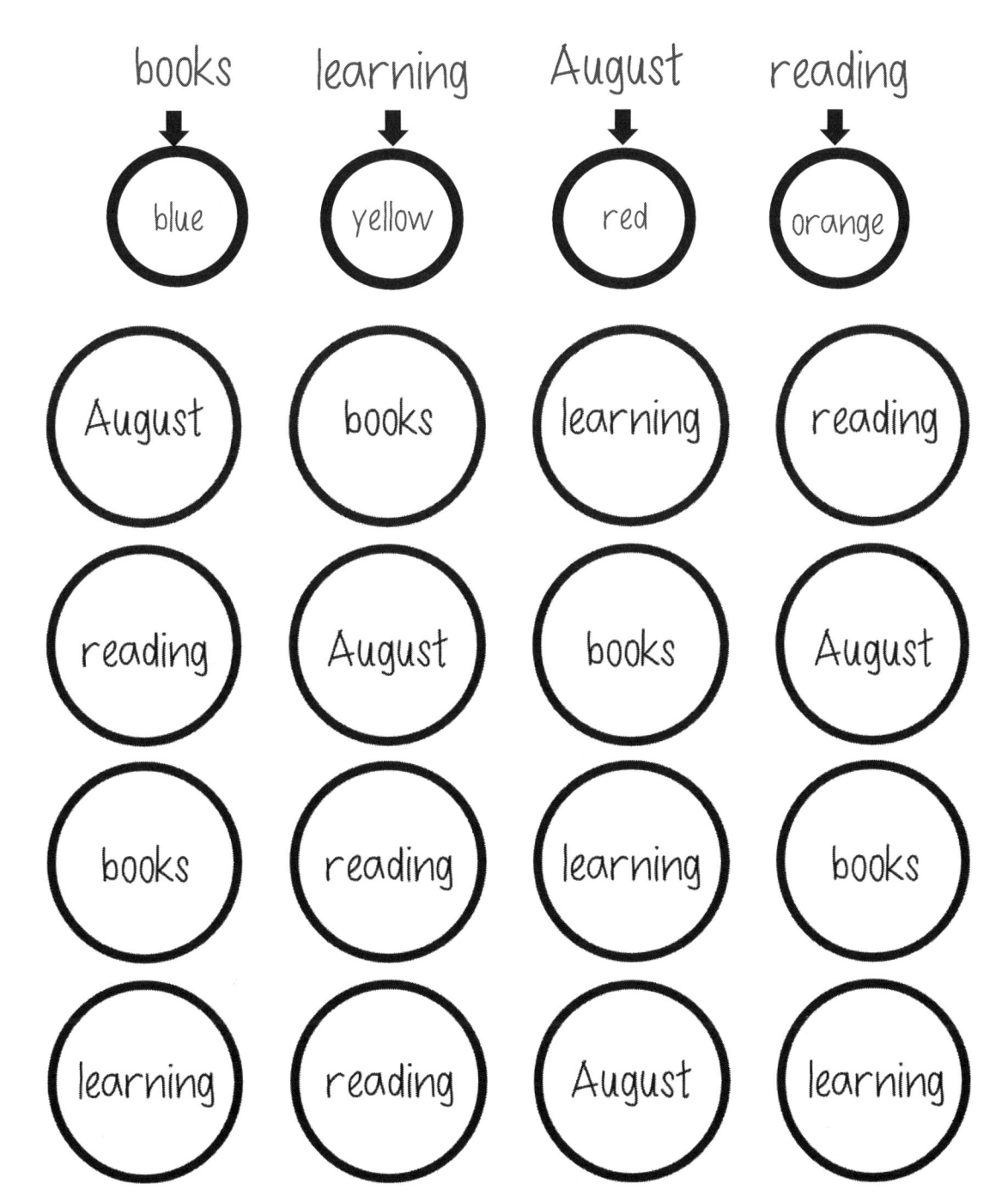

books	learning	August	reading
↓	↓	↓	↓
blue	yellow	red	orange

August	books	learning	reading
reading	August	books	August
books	reading	learning	books
learning	reading	August	learning

Morning Work for Teens

Name:

27

August

Trace the word.

smile

Color in the 4 pictures that show someone smiling.

Definition:

to form your face to show that you are happy.

Directions: Circle the correct word that matches the definition..

| spill | smile | smit |

Smile
Draw a picture that shows someone smiling

WRITE IT!!!

smile

Morning Work for Teens

Name: _____   29   August

Color in the words.

Back to School

Cut and paste the sayings to show back to school items.

Eat an apple for snack.

Writing my name.

Take notes in my notebook.

Put on my backpack.

Morning Work for Teens

31

August

Name:_____

Trace the words that say empathy.

friendly

friendly

found

friendly

fame

find

friendly

Mark the word
friendly

friendly	find	frosting
find	friendly	falling
friendly	findings	friendly
phase	friendly	friendly
filling	find	fun
friendly	phasing	friendly

Friendly Definition
Directions: Mark the correct definition.

☐ To keep someone far away.

☐ To welcome and be kind to someone.

WRITE IT!!!
friendly

_____
- - - - - - - - - - - - - -
_____

Mark the picture of the student who is being friendly.

Morning Work for Teens

Name:

33

August

Trace the word.

August

Count the numbers. Trace the numbers.

1 2 3 4 5 6 7 8 9 10 11 12
13 14 15 16 17 18 19 20 21
22 23 24 25 26 27 28 29
30 31

"August is a month of sunshine, fun, and getting ready for school!"

Ice Cream Day:
Count the ice cream cones. Color every other ice cream cone.

Question:
How many days are in August?

Directions: Circle the correct answer.

| ten | thirty-one | five |

What do students ride in August to go to school?

backpack   bus

Morning Work for Teens

Name: _____

August

Back to School Vocabulary

Directions: Match the word cards to the same word card.

friends	notebook
paper	students
school crossing sign	books
school supplies	desk

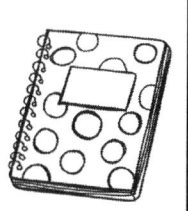

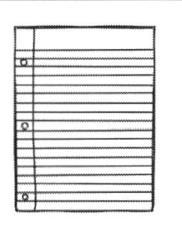

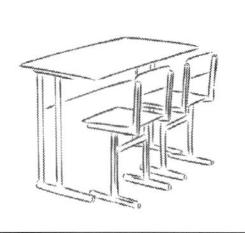

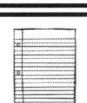

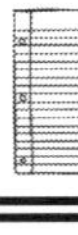

friends  | notebook 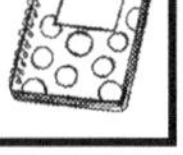 | desk 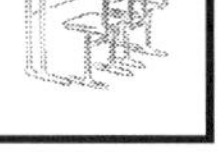
paper | students  | school supplies 
school crossing sign  | books

Morning Work for Teens

37

August

Name: _____

Students in Action

Directions: Match the action to the picture.

| paint | play |
| work | read |

Morning Work for Teens

39

August

Name:_____

Back to School Match

Directions: Use pencil, string or thread to connect the pictures that match.

Morning Work for Teens 41 August
Name: _____

Letter of Approval
Directions: Fill in the blanks to finish the letter.

_____
Date

Good Morning,

   The month is _____. We are back in _____. There are many things to do here. One of my favorite things to do at school is _____. I am _____ to be back at school.

Signed,
_____

August	paint	music class	happy
September	write	eat lunch	sad
school	play with friends	use the computer	thankful

Morning Work for Teens

Name: _____

43

August

Letter of Approval

Directions: Fill in the blanks to finish the letter.

_____
Date

Good Morning,

    The month is _____. We are back in _____. There are many things to do here. One of my favorite things to do at school is _____. I am _____ to be back at school.

Signed,
_____

August	paint	music class	happy
September	write	eat lunch	sad
school	play with friends	use the computer	thankful

Morning Work for Teens

Name:

45

August

Back to School Shuffle

Directions: Mark the same.

Morning Work for Teens 47 August

Name:

Directions: Mark the correct answer.

- ○ backpack
- ○ book

- ○ shoe
- ○ notebook

- ○ bookcase
- ○ globe

- ○ pencil
- ○ button

- ○ box
- ○ table

- ○ chair
- ○ desk

Morning Work for Teens

Name:_____

49

August

Trace the word.

learning

learning

Place a check mark by each phrase that show ways to learn.

☐ Dog learning to sit

☐ Kid learning to read

☐ Teens learning to drive

☐ Babies crawling

☐ A parrot saying hello

Mark the word learning.

ton   even   learning

learning   can   speaking

gift   looking   learning

Definition:
To gain knowledge through study.

Directions: Circle the correct word.

| giving | learning | singing |

WRITE IT !!!

learning

_____

- -

_____

learning <u>begins</u> with which letter?

w   l   g

Morning Work for Teens

51

August

Name:

Trace the word.

friend

Mark the word friend.

friend   bus   enemy

bully   bag   friend

teacher   friend   book

friend

Definition:
A person you like talking to, like playing games with or like being around.

Directions: Circle the correct word.

| palace | friend | foe |

Sounds Like...
Directions: Mark the rhyming words.

friend   look   send   crate

mend   empty   bend   lend

WRITE IT!!!
friend

Mark the picture that is different.

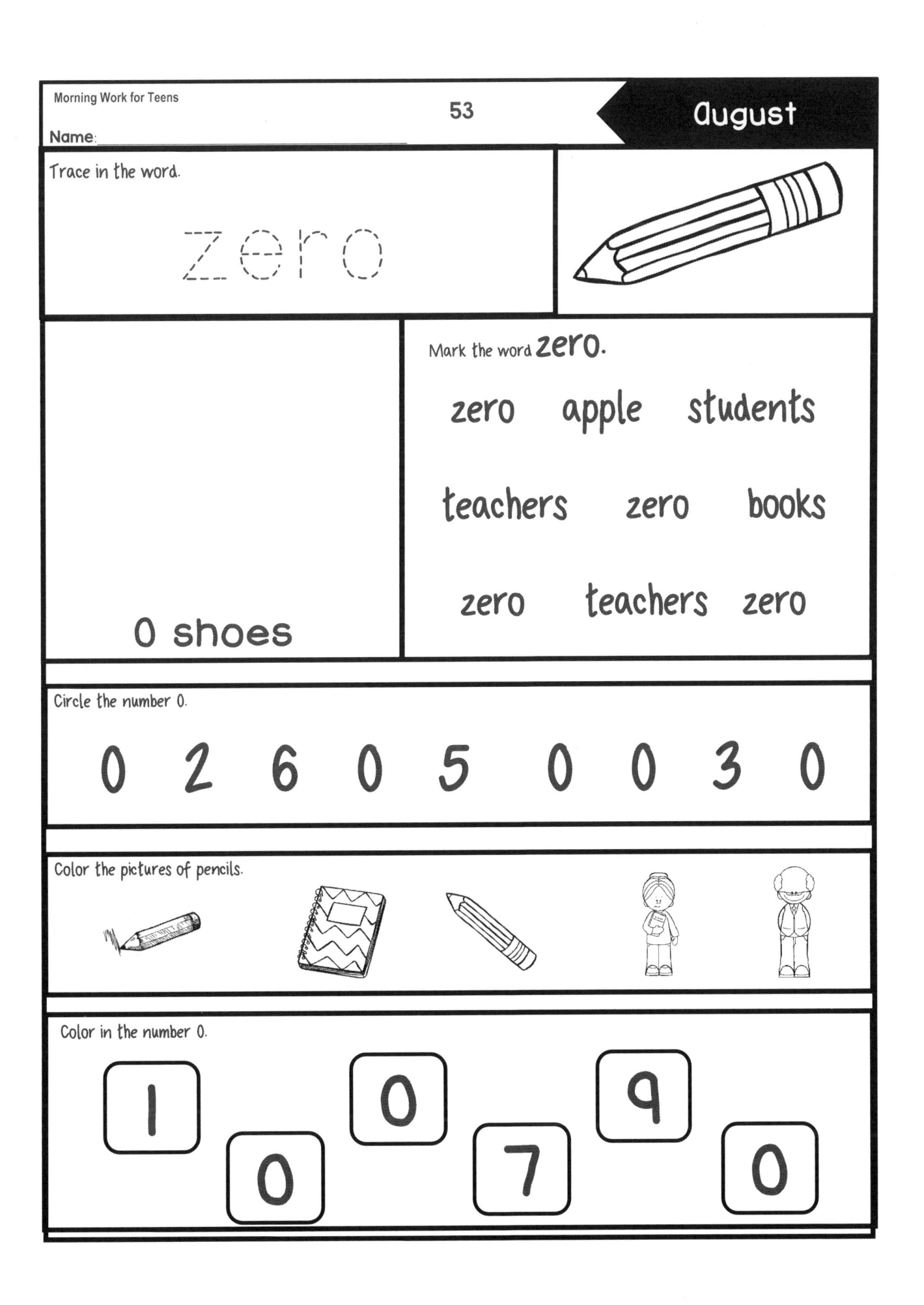

Morning Work for Teens 53 august

Name:

Trace in the word.

zero

Mark the word zero.

zero   apple   students

teachers   zero   books

zero   teachers   zero

0 shoes

Circle the number 0.

0   2   6   0   5   0   0   3   0

Color the pictures of pencils.

Color in the number 0.

1   0   9

0   7   0

September

Morning Work for Teens with Special Needs

For 6th – 12th grade students with significant special needs

Autism Classroom

Morning Work for Teens

57

September

Name:

September Vocabulary

Directions: Match the definition to the word.

September		school	
teacher		rule	
courtesy		flexible	
schedule		Golden Rule	

An act of kindness.

Treat others like you want them to treat you.

Ready and able to change or bend without breaking.

A plan or set of activities.

The month between August and October.

The instructor in a classroom.

A place for learning.

A list of things you should and should not do.

Morning Work for Teens 59 September

Name:

Bingo Marker Number Search
Directions: September has 30 days. Dot the number 30 on the MP3 Player.

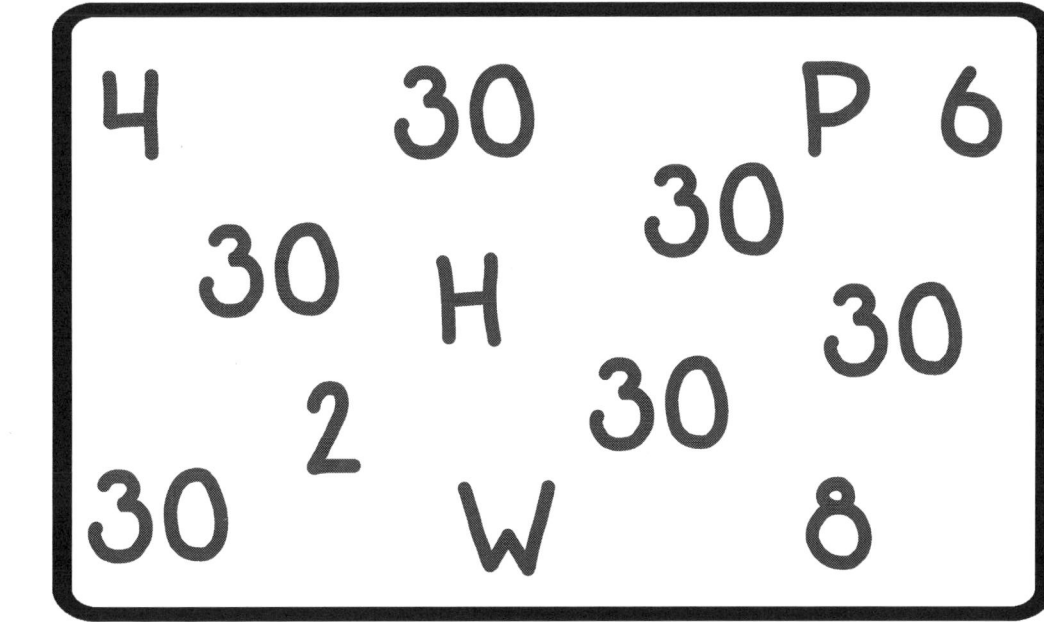

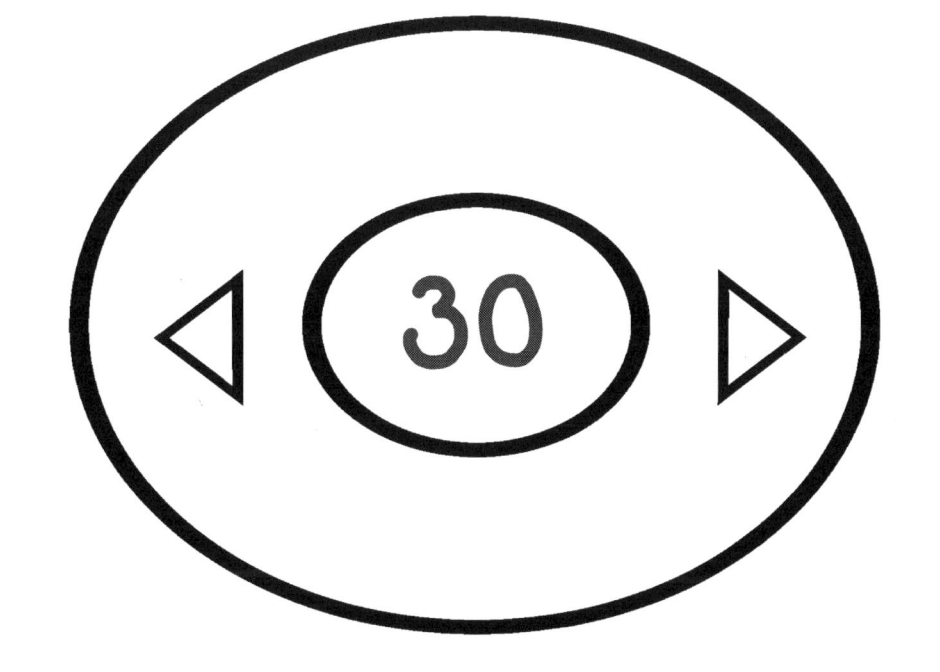

4 30 P 6
30 30
30 H
   30
2 30
30 W 8

30

Morning Work for Teens

Name: _____

61

September

School Sorts

Directions: Sort the pictures in the correct box.

Morning Work for Teens
Name:

63

September

Girls and Boys

Directions: Cut and paste the boys in Room 2 and the girls in Room 5.

Room 2

Room 5

Morning Work for Teens

Name: _____

September

Nature Hunt Report

Directions: Gather 3 or 4 leaves. Choose one leaf from the bunch. Cut and paste an answer about the leaf you choose.

Color:	Size:

Shape:	Opinion:

red	circle
green	triangle
brown	rectangle
yellow	oval
orange	leaf-shaped
large	I like my leaf.
medium	My leaf is so-so.
small	I do not like my leaf.

Morning Work for Teens

Name:

67

September

Cutting Practice and Choice Making

Directions: Cut out the two picture frames. Cut out only 2 pictures below. Glue in your favorite pictures onto the inside of each frame.

Morning Work for Teens

Name:

69

September

Word Search

Directions: Circle the words.

school

| school | school | take | are | school | school | think |
| day | school | we | here | school | school | date | fill |

autumn

| fall | autumn | spring | autumn | winter | give | many |
| autumn | to | finish | autumn | letter | blank | autumn |

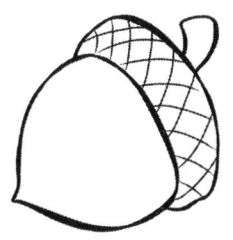

acorn

| acorn | acorn | acorn | apple | first | acorn | case |
| acorn | marker | pen | acorn | staple | acorn | acorn |

Morning Work for Teens   71   September
Name:

Doodle Art
Directions: Use a marker or colored pencil to color in the design.

Morning Work for Teens

Name:_____

73

September

Trace and Write

Directions: Trace the numbers.
Write your own in the box.

1 1 1 1

2 2 2 2 2 2 2

3 3 3 3 3 3 3

4 4 4 4 4 4 4

5 5 5 5 5 5 5

Morning Work for Teens 75 September

Name:_____

Directions: Mark the correct answer.

- ○ writing
- ○ skiing
- ○ walking

- ○ dancing
- ○ reading
- ○ crying

- ○ talking
- ○ running
- ○ fishing

- ○ cooking
- ○ sitting
- ○ standing

- ○ painting
- ○ eating
- ○ raising hand

- ○ jumping
- ○ drawing
- ○ typing

Morning Work for Teens

Name: _____

77

September

Students in Action

Directions: Match the action to the picture.

| kicking | listening |
| walking | skating |

Morning Work for Teens

Name: _____

79

September

Apple Words and Phrases

Directions: Match the words to the picture.

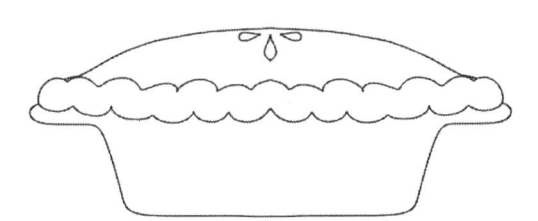

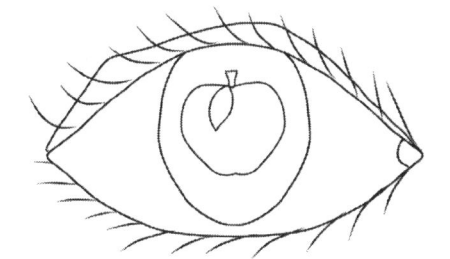

apple of my eye

apple pie

basket of apples

apple tree

Morning Work for Teens

Name:

81

September

Teens in School Match

Directions: Use pencil, string or thread to connect the pictures that match.

Morning Work for Teens

Name: _____

A Letter to a Friend

Directions: Fill in the blanks to finish the letter.

Date _____

Hi Friend,

    It is _____. Students are back in _____. Teachers are here too. I am _____ to be back at school. This is because I like to _____ when I am at school.

Signed,

_____

August	home	have music class	happy
September	work	eat lunch	sad
school	play with friends	use the computer	excited

Morning Work for Teens
Name:_____

85

September

A Letter to a Friend
Directions: Fill in the blanks to finish the letter.

Date_____

Hi Friend,

   It is _____. Students are back in _____. Teachers are here too. I am _____ to be back at school. This is because I like to _____ when I am at school.

Signed,

_____

August	home	have music class	happy
September	work	eat lunch	sad
school	play with friends	use the computer	excited

Morning Work for Teens

Name: _____

September

Back to School Social Vocabulary

Directions: Mark the same.

courtesy

courtesy   bat   enemy

bully   courtesy   fry

teach   talk   courtesy

flexible

suit   flexible   you

flexible   bag   friend

sing   flexible   bat

golden rule

golden rule   tree   sharp

born   golden rule   of

pit   stop   golden rule

rules

letter   speaker   rules

pencil   rules   month

rules   phone   book

Morning Work for Teens

89

September

Name:_____

Trace the word.

golden rule

Color in the pictures that rhyme with rule.

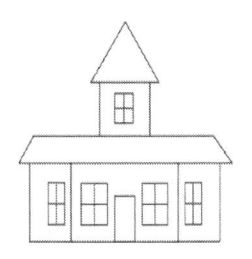

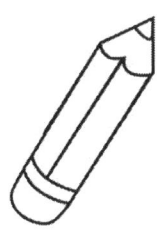

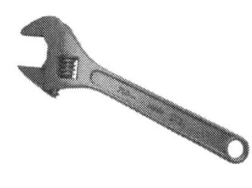

Definition:

Treat others like you want them to treat you.

Directions: Circle the correct word that matches the definition..

| golden rule | social | courage |

WRITE IT !!!

golden rule

Fight or Play...

Mark the picture that shows the golden rule.

Morning Work for Teens
Name:_____
91
September

Trace the word.
courtesy | courtesy

Mark the word courtesy.

dot   talk   courtesy

share   courtesy   square

thought   kind   courtesy

Definition:
An act of kindness.

Directions: Circle the correct word.

| case | courtesy | apple |

WRITE IT !!!
courtesy

Courtesy begins with which letter?

f   c   y

Morning Work for Teens   93   **September**

Name:_____

Color in the word.

flexible

Is the person being flexible?

- ○ Yes ○ No
- ○ Yes ○ No
- ○ Yes ○ No
- ○ Yes ○ No
- ○ Yes ○ No

Find the work below.

flexible

flexible   **rigid**   camp

write   tell   flexible

Fill in the circle for the correct word:

○ eating

Ready and able to change or bend without breaking.

○ flexible

○ rigid

WRITE IT !!!
flexible

_____
_ _ _ _ _ _ _ _ _ _ _ _ _ _
_____

Mark the picture that shows flexible.

Morning Work for Teens

95

September

Name:_____

Trace the word.

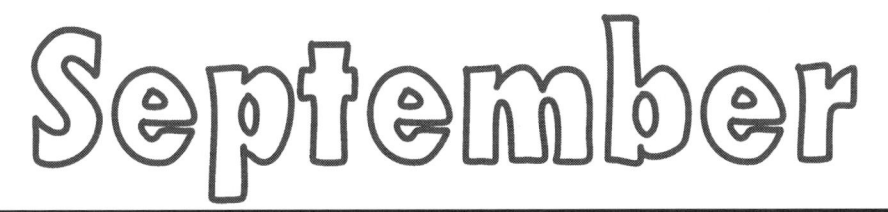

September

Count the numbers. Circle the last number.

1 2 3 4 5 6 7 8 9 10
11 12 13 14 15 16 17 18
19 20 21 22 23 24 25
26 27 28 29 30

Question:

How many days are in September?

Which number is 30?

7   30

Directions: Circle the correct answer.

| thirty | nine | seven |

WRITE IT !!!
thirty

Which picture shows 30 notebooks ?

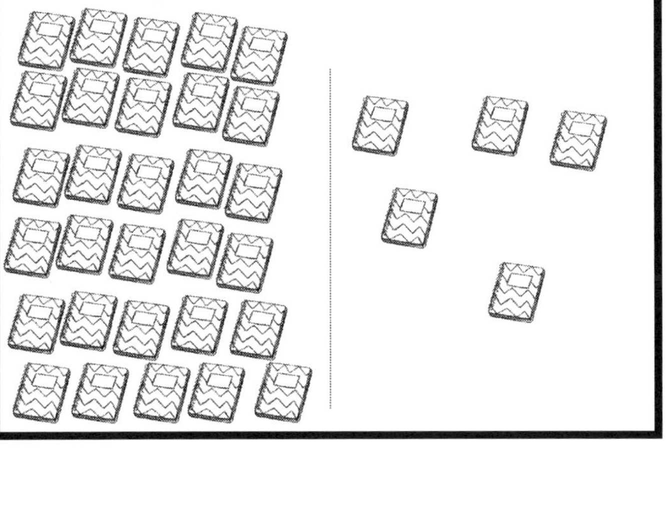

Morning Work for Teens

97

September

Name:

Trace the word.

school

school

Mark the word school.

one   bus   school

school   bag   type

teacher   school   book

What Sounds Like School?

Directions: Mark the rhyming words.

cool   like   turn

mend   spool   pencil

WRITE IT !!!
school

Mark the picture that is different.

Morning Work for Teens

Name: _____

qq

September

Trace in the word.

one

Around My School

Mark the word **library**.

library	book	library
pants	library	tan
sat	library	book

1 library

Circle the number 1.

1   2   2   1   1   3   1   1   3

Color the pictures of libraries.

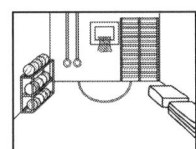

October

Morning Work for Teens with Special Needs

For 6th - 12th grade students with significant special needs

Autism Classroom

Morning Work for Teens

Name:_____

103

October

October Vocabulary

Directions: Match the definition to the word.

October		autumn	
office		football	
kind		play	
game		cooperation	

- Being nice to others.
- Working together.
- A fun activity with rules.
- The season between spring and winter.
- The month between September and November.
- To take part in an activity for fun.
- A game played with a ball, a helmet and a jersey.
- The part of the school with the principal's desk.

Morning Work for Teens

Name:_____

105

October

October Number Search

Directions: October has 31 days. Mark the number 31.

4 31 31
31 8 5
31 6
45 30
2 31
12 3
31 36 8
31 3

Morning Work for Teens

Name:

107

October

Fall Sports Sorts

Directions: Sort the pictures in the correct box.

Morning Work for Teens

Name:_____

109

October

What Do You Think?

Directions: Cut and paste what you think best tells the story in the picture.

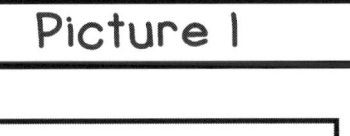

Picture 1

Picture 2

- He is looking at the stars.
- He is angry.
- She is happy with her new hair style
- She is doing a science experiment.

Morning Work for Teens

Name:_____

October

Technology Report

Directions: Cut and paste your opinion about each piece of technology.

Tablets are the best.
I like my iPad.
Tablets are too big.
I love my computer.
Computers have cool games.
Computer games are boring.
No thanks.
Yes. This is so fun.

This thing is great.
The phone is too small.
I want my own phone.
Phone apps are fun.
Noise hurts my ears.
I hate things on my ears.
Headphones are cool.
I do not like my TV.

Morning Work for Teens

Name:_____

113

October

Cutting Practice and Coupons
Directions: Cut out the two coupons.

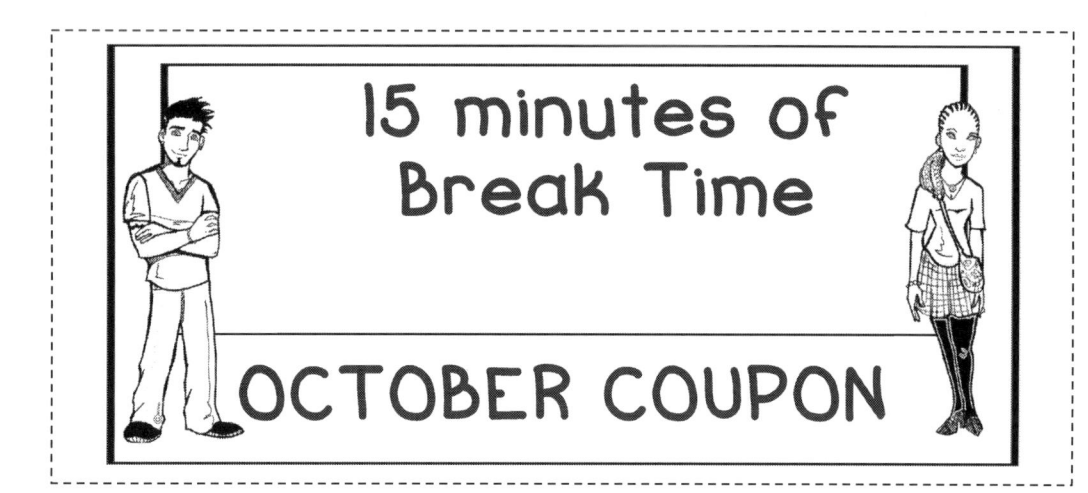

15 minutes of Break Time

OCTOBER COUPON

15 minutes of Tablet Time

OCTOBER COUPON

Morning Work for Teens

Name:_____

115

October

Trace and Write
Directions: Trace the words. Write your own in the box.

First

Next

Last

Morning Work for Teens

Name:_____

117

October

What Does This Mean?

Match the picture and the definition to the saying.

Cry over spilled milk.	A fish out of water.

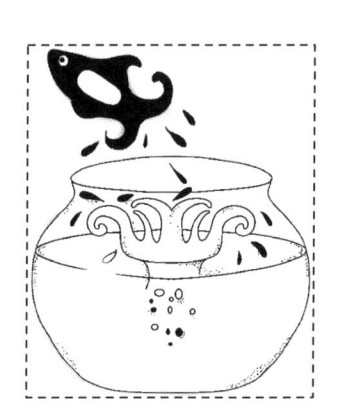

Feeling uncomfortable or feeling unable to do something.

Over-reacting to a small problem that has already happened.

Morning Work for Teens
Name:_____

119

October

Directions: Mark the correct answer.

- ○ orange
- ○ spider
- ○ man

- ○ run
- ○ pumpkin
- ○ black

- ○ candy
- ○ cotton
- ○ coat

- ○ speaker
- ○ dog
- ○ cat

- ○ sand
- ○ doll
- ○ scarecrow

- ○ boat
- ○ bat
- ○ back

Morning Work for Teens

Name:_____

121

October

Wild Science
Directions: Mark the same.

Mark the same.

Mark the same.

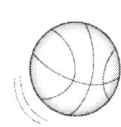

Mark the same.

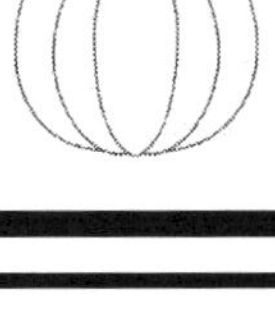

Morning Work for Teens
Name:_____

123

October

Directions: Draw a line to the things that are usually black. Draw a line to the things that are usually orange.

orange

black

Morning Work for Teens
Name:_____   125   October

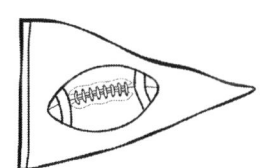

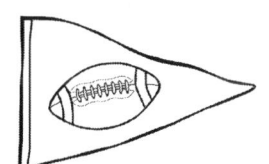

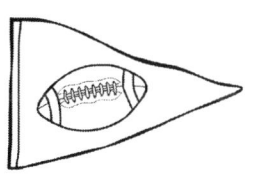

Go Team !!! Hole Punch

Day 1: Cut on the dotted line. Laminate or place clear tape over both sides.
Day 2: Cut out the gray area. Hole punch the dark circles.
Day 3: Tie string through the holes to create a Pom-Pom.

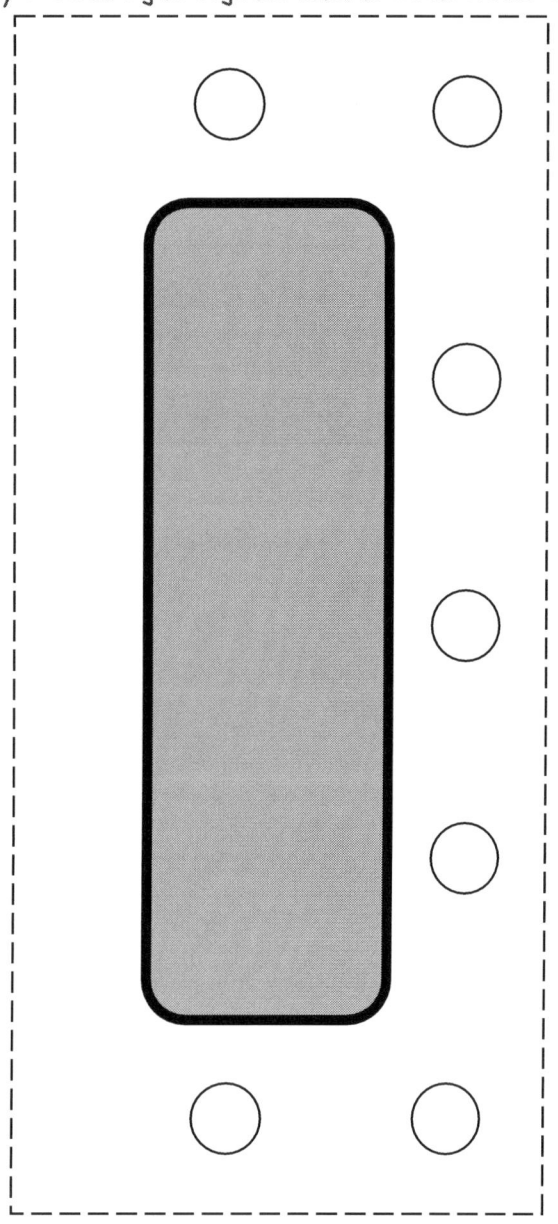

Morning Work for Teens 127 October

Name:_____

Football
Bingo Marker Search
Directions: Dot the things you see at a football game.

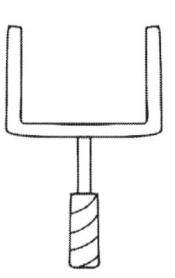

Morning Work for Teens
Name:_____

129

October

Trace Words

Directions: Trace over these words then draw a line to match them to the definition.

football

jersey

helmet

cleats

goal post

Morning Work for Teens

Name:_____

131

October

Cutting Practice
Directions: Cut out the triangle shapes.

Morning Work for Teens

Name:_____

133

October

Trace the word.

October

Count the numbers. Circle the last number.

1 2 3 4 5 6 7 8 9 10
11 12 13 14 15 16 17 18
19 20 21 22 23 24 25
26 27 28 29 30 31

Question:

How many days are in October?

Directions: Circle the correct answer.

| thirty | thirty one | three |

Which number is 31 ?

7   31

WRITE IT !!!

thirty one

Which words say October ?

October   September   October
    October
November   December
    January
October   October   March

Morning Work for Teens
Name:_____

135

October

October Social Vocabulary
Directions: Mark the same.

kind
sort	kind	yes
bull	child	kind
reach	**kind**	**court**

play
suit	play	you
able	play	end
sing	**flexible**	**play**

game
rule	tree	game
born	game	it
pit	**game**	**gold**

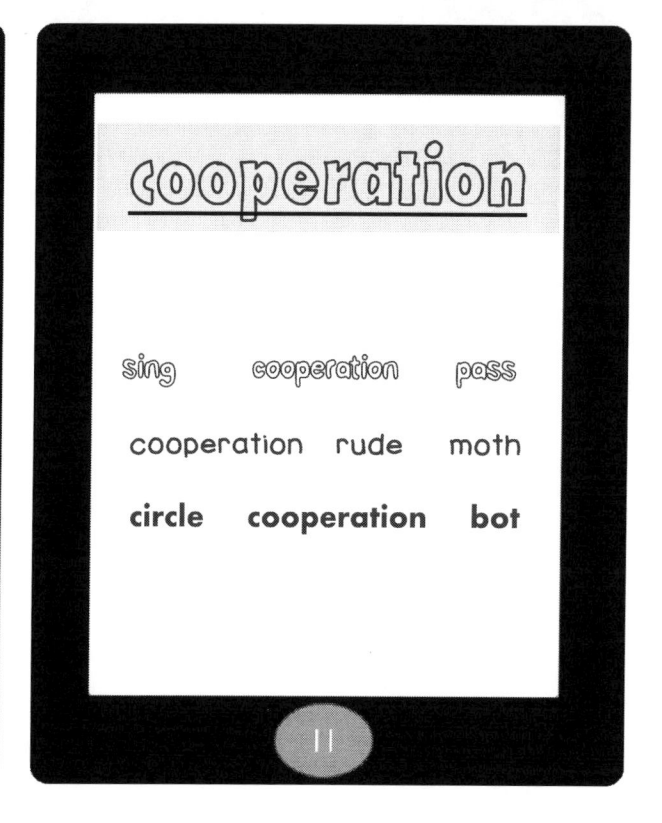

cooperation
sing	cooperation	pass
cooperation	rude	moth
circle	**cooperation**	**bot**

Morning Work for Teens

Name: _____

137

October

Emotions Apps

Directions: Point to the letters on the keyboard to spell the words.

- KIND
- CALM
- RELAXED
- HAPPY
- CONTENT
- FRIENDLY

Morning Work for Teens

Name:_____

139

October

Trace the word.

point

Point to the following numbers on the keypad below.

3   8   7   1   4

Circle the word "point" below.

point   orange   point   point   point
         black
point   picture   paint

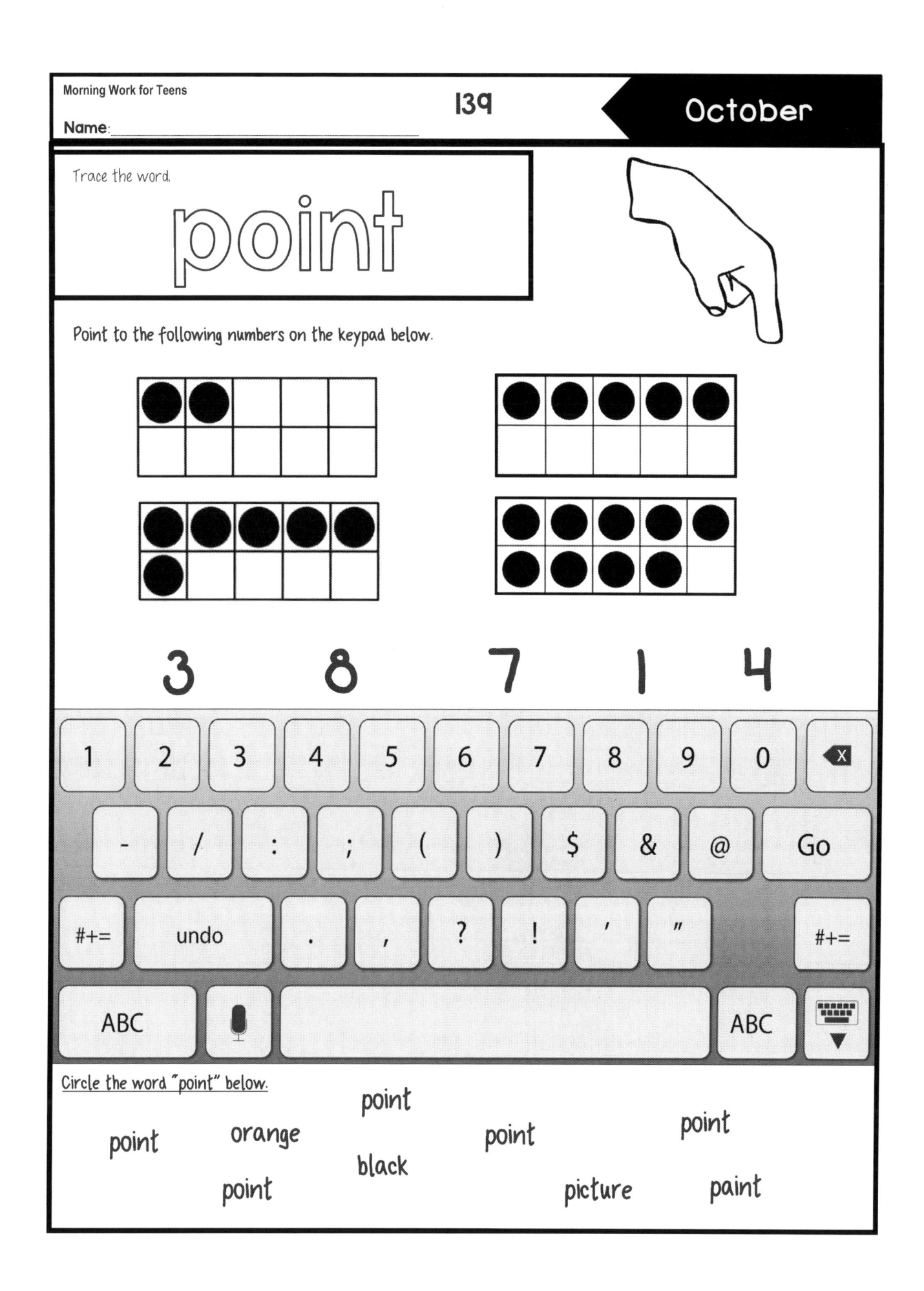

Morning Work for Teens

Name:_____

141

October

Trace the word.

calm

Circle the words that say "calm" in this picture.

Dear Sam,
Back in the summer, I was calm at the beach. Mainly because the ocean was so calm.

STAY CALM AND HAVE FUN

CALM

Definition:

Peaceful or relaxed.

Directions: Circle the correct word that matches the definition..

| adversity | calm | empathy |

WRITE IT !!!

calm

Mark the picture that shows someone being calm.

Calm ?

Morning Work for Teens

Name:_____

143

October

Trace in the word.

two

Around My School

Mark the word office.

three	office	paper
phone	office	speaker
office	library	shell

2 plants

Circle the number 2.
1 2 2 1 1 3 1 1 3 4
7 5 6 2 2 9 2 2 1 5

Color the pictures with plants.

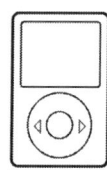

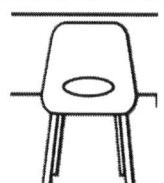

Morning Work for Teens

Name:_____

145

October

Trace the word.

play

play

Mark the word play.

play	play	run
play	drive	play
play	play	walk

Draw a line to the pictures that show work and the pictures that show play.

Work

Play

Morning Work for Teens

Name:

147

October

game

Mark the word.

| game | game | same | game |
| name | game | game | fame |

Color the word.

game

Mark the word.

○ same

○ game

○ game

Paste the word.

game

Use it in a sentence.

I want to play that ⬚ .

Cut and paste in the sentence above.

Cut and paste in the right column above.

game

game

game

game

Morning Work for Teens
Name:_____

149

October

Trace the word.

Cooperation

Draw a line to the same letter in the word cooperation.

| c | o | o | p | e | r | a | t | i | o | n |

| p | o | c | a | o | r | i | e | n | o | t |

Definition:

The process of working together with someone.

Directions: Circle the correct word that matches the definition.

| fight | count | cooperation |

TRACE IT !!!

cooperation

Cooperation at Work

Mark the pictures that show cooperation.

November

Morning Work for Teens with Special Needs

For 6th – 12th grade students with significant special needs.

Morning Work for Teens

153

November

Name:_____

Trace in the word.

Veteran's Day

Mark the word **veteran**.

veteran   veteran   gray

veteran   hero   veteran

veteran   veteran   vote

Veteran's Day

Circle the letter V.

V   M   V   V   V   D   V   V   H

Underline the pictures that show a veteran solider.

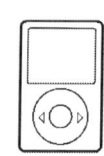

Morning Work for Teens
Name:_____

155

November

Election Day Vocabulary

Directions: Match the word cards to the same word card.

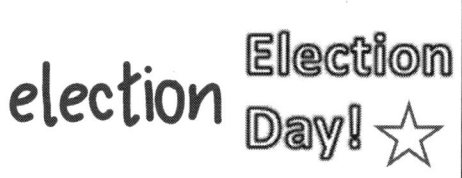

vote 	ballot box 
election	check mark 
Tuesday 	pick 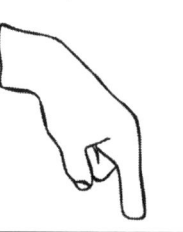
Republican 	Democrat 

---

vote | ballot box | Republican
election | check mark | Democrat
Tuesday | pick

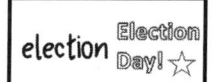

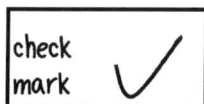

Morning Work for Teens
Name:_____

157

November

Election Day Vocabulary

Directions: Match the definition to the word.

vote		ballot box	
election		check mark	
Tuesday		pick	
Republican		Democrat	

- A box to hold votes.
- Political party whose symbol is a donkey.
- The day after Monday.
- To formally express your choice for a candidate.
- A mark used to signal that something is finished or chosen.
- Political party whose symbol is an elephant.
- A process to collect and tally votes.
- To choose.

Morning Work for Teens

Name:

159

November

November Number Search
Directions: November has 30 days. Mark the number 30.

8   30   30   1
31   5   3
6
30
30
2   30
17   39
30   36
31   1

Morning Work for Teens

Name:_____

161

November

American Education Week

Directions: These twins love American Education Week. Can you locate the twins and mark them?

Mark the same.

Mark the same.

Mark the same.

Morning Work for Teens

Name:_____

163

November

Football Shuffle

Directions: Mark the picture *and* word that is the same as the picture in the circle.

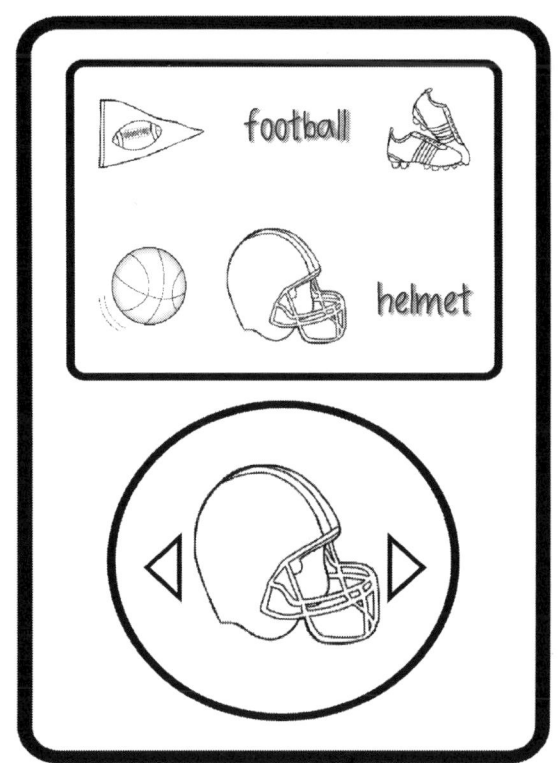

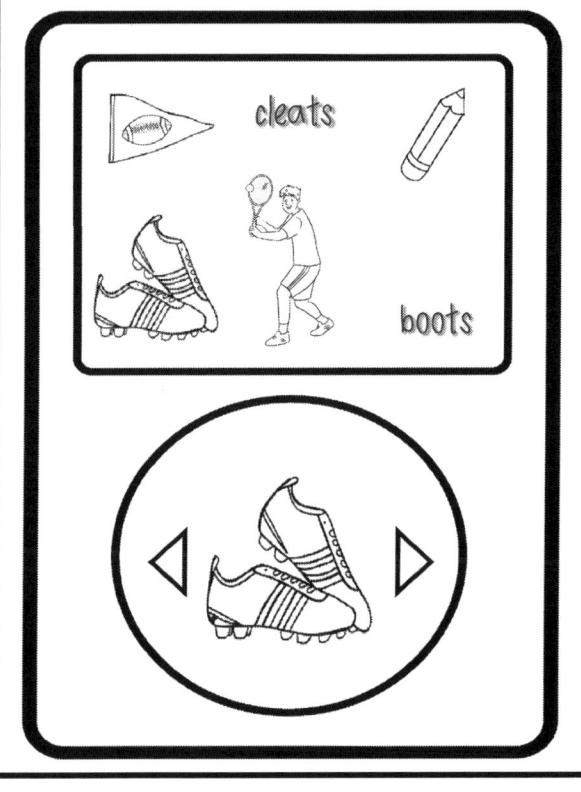

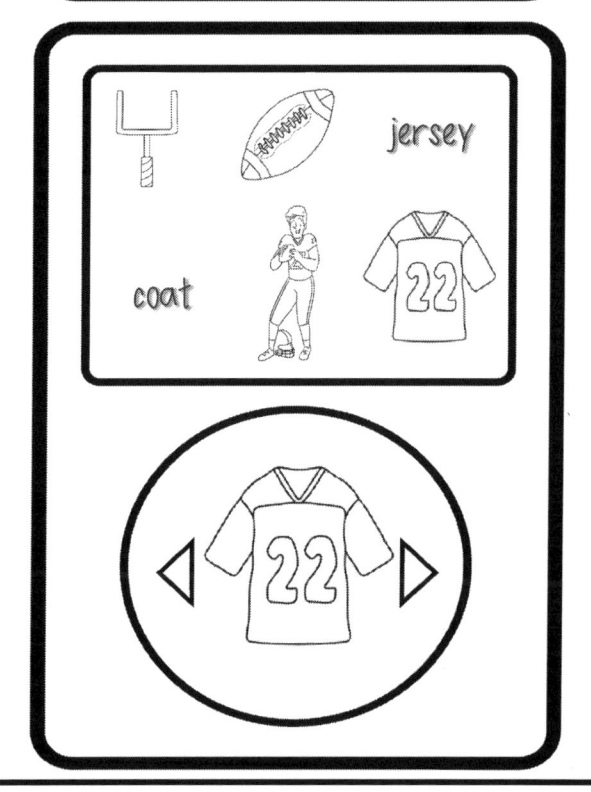

football player

tennis

football

helmet

cleats

boots

jersey

coat

Morning Work for Teens

Name:_____

165

November

Build a Sentence

Directions: Choose the strips below to build 3 sentences.

1.
2.
3.

Beginning

- November
- This week
- Football
- This school year

Ending

- is a great month.
- is a boring month.
- will be fun.
- will be difficult for me.
- is my favorite sport.
- is not interesting to me.
- has been fun so far.
- has been hard.

Morning Work for Teens

Name:_____

November

Punctuation Match

Directions: Mark the box to show if this is a statement or a question.

? . ? . ?

This month is November.	. statement	? question
Is this month November?	. statement	? question
Who is playing in the football game?	. statement	? question
I am playing in the football game.	. statement	? question
Are you going to Thanksgiving dinner?	. statement	? question
She is going to Thanksgiving dinner.	. statement	? question

Morning Work for Teens
Name:_____

169

November

November Social Vocabulary
Directions: Mark the same.

thoughtful

skill   thoughtful   mean

nice   kind   thoughtful

calm   talk   thoughtful

persistence

toad   flexible   persistence

persistence   bag   fry

thing   persistence   at

share

type   tree   share

box   share   for

hit   top   share

keep trying

letter   keep trying   rude

pencil   keep trying   on

rules   keep trying   be

Morning Work for Teens
Name:_____
171
November

turkey

Mark the word.

| bag | turkey | light | menu | turkey | then |
| turkey | eat | show | turkey | box | how |

Paste the word.

turkey

Use a line to match the picture to the word.

turkey

on

shirt

Mark the word.

○ turkey

○ top

○ turkey

Write the word on the line.
_____

turkey

Cut only the word turkey. Then paste in the right column.

turkey

turkey

turkey

phone

Morning Work for Teens

Name:_____

173

November

Thanksgiving in Action

Directions: Match the action to the picture.

play

eat

visit

cook

watch

watch

eat

visit

cook

play

Morning Work for Teens

Name:_____

175

November

Thanksgiving Vocabulary: Mark the correct answer.

○ family
○ skiing
○ tree

○ soap
○ drink
○ eating utensils

○ dinner
○ store
○ stapler

○ turkey
○ bat
○ wolf

○ painting
○ eating
○ friends

○ lemon
○ pumpkin
○ apple

Morning Work for Teens

Name:_____

177

November

Menu Report
Directions: Cut and paste your opinion about each food.

Mashed Potatoes	Gravy

Turkey	Peas

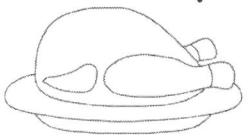

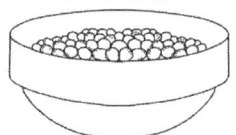

Mashed potatoes are my favorite food.

Yuck, mashed potatoes!

No thanks.

I love this food.

Turkey is the best.

I don't like turkey meat.

This tastes yucky.

Yes. This is food I like.

Peas are disgusting.

Peas are tasty food.

I love peas.

I hate peas.

Gravy is good.

I hate food that is runny.

No gravy for me, please.

I do not like this.

Morning Work for Teens

Name:_____

179

November

Turkey Trot

Directions: Choose a name for each picture. Cut it out and glue it onto the picture you choose.

Tom Turkey

Yoga Turkey

Mr. and Mrs. Turkey

Happy Thanksgiving Turkey

Morning Work for Teens

Name:_____

181

November

Family Dinner Sorts
Directions: Sort the pictures in the correct box.

Morning Work for Teens
Name:_____
183
November

November

Mark the abbreviation for November. (Nov.)

Nov.	Oct.	Feb.	Nov.
Aug.	Nov.	Nov.	Dec.

Mark the word.

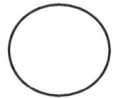

○ November

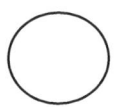

○ August

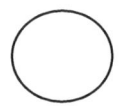

○ November

Write the word below.

November

Paste the word.

November

Cut out only the word November. Then, paste in the right column.

eat | November

November | November

Morning Work for Teens

Name:_____

185

November

Trace the word.

November

Count the numbers. Circle the first and last number.

1 2 3 4 5 6 7 8 9 10
11 12 13 14 15 16 17 18
19 20 21 22 23 24 25
26 27 28 29 30

Question:

How many days are in November?

Directions: Circle the correct answer.

| thirty-one | thirty | twenty |

Which number is 30?

7   30

Which number is more? Underline the number that shows more.

WRITE IT !!!
thirty

_____

_ _ _ _ _ _ _ _ _ _ _ _ _ _ _

_____

Which words say November ?

November   August   November
          October   December
November
       January   March
April   November

Morning Work for Teens
Name:_____

187

November

Trace the word.

share

Color in the pictures that rhyme with share.

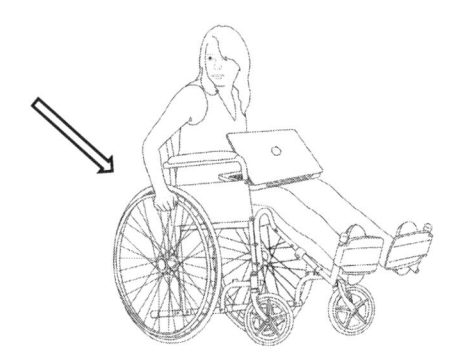

Definition:

To use something that is yours with another person.

Directions: Circle the correct word that matches the definition..

| share | five | ready |

WRITE IT !!!

share

Sharing...

Mark the 3 pictures that show sharing.

Morning Work for Teens
Name:_____

189

November

share

Mark the word.

| keep share share share |
| share share stop share |

Paste the word.

share

Color the word.

share

Mark the word.
○ share
○ stop
○ sign

Use it in a sentence.

Please [_____] with others.

Cut and paste in the sentence above.

Cut and paste in the right column above.

share

share   share   share

Morning Work for Teens 191 November
Name:_____

Color in the word.

thoughtful

Is this being thoughtful?

○ Yes ○ No

○ Yes ○ No

○ Yes ○ No

○ Yes ○ No

○ Yes ○ No

Find the word below.

thoughtful

mean   **thoughtful**   cat

thoughtful   so   upset

Fill in the circle for the correct word:
○ thoughtful

Caring about other people.
○ angry

○ selfish

WRITE IT !!!
thoughtful

Mark the letter t.

s   t   e   t   l   s   b
h   t   p   g   d   f
o   t   o   a   y   t
t   z   t   p   l   t

Morning Work for Teens
Name:_____

193

November

Trace the word in your favorite colors.

Persistence

Draw a line to the same letter in the word persistence.

| p | e | r | s | i | s | t | e | n | c | e |

| p | s | c | e | e | r | i | e | n | s | t |

Definition:

The ability to continue working at a task even when it is difficult.

Directions: Circle the correct word that matches the definition..

| caring | share | persistence |

TRACE IT !!!

persistence

Sayings with Persistence

Mark the words that show persistence.

Keep trying.

I will try again.

I give up.

Morning Work for Teens

Name:_____

195

November

Trace the words.

keep trying

Mark the word try.

try	try	run
play	try	try
stop	try	try

What can they say to keep trying?

Draw a line to the pictures that show what the teens can say to get the task done.

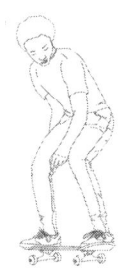

| I can get this answer if I just use the steps the teacher told me. | I am tired, but I can make this goal if I just keep trying. | Skateboarding may be hard, but if I keep trying, I can do it. | I am going to swing this bat until I hit that ball. |

Morning Work for Teens

Name:_____

197

November

Trace in the word.

three

Around My School

Mark the word **gym**.

gym	office	gym
gym	gym	speaker
nurse	gym	gym

3 basketballs players

Circle the number 3.

1 3 9 2 3 3 1 3 3 7
8 3 5 3 2 4 3 2 1 5

Color the pictures of a gym.

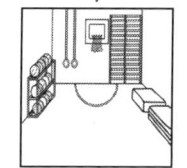

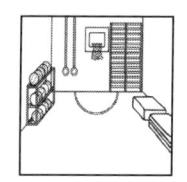

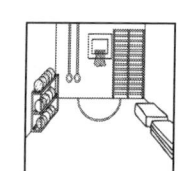

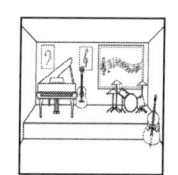

Morning Work for Teens

Name:_____

199

November

What Do You Think?

Directions: Cut and paste what you think best tells the story in the picture.

Picture 1

Picture 2

- A basketball game.
- A trip to the beach.
- A family dinner.
- A snow storm.

Thank you...

Thank you for purchasing Morning Work for Teens with Special Needs.

Other items from AutismClassroom.com include:

-Teen's Edition Social Skills Printables Workbook
-Time Saving Tips for Busy Autism Classroom Teachers
-Time-Saving Visuals for an Autism Support Classroom
-Executive Functioning Skills Printables Workbook
-Alphabet Tracing Book
-How to Set Up a Classroom for Students with Autism (Audio and Paperback)

The Morning Work for Teens Series

Book 1 - Morning Work for Teens with Special Needs Workbook (August, September, October, & November)

Book 2 - Morning Work for Teens with Special Needs Workbook (December, January, February, & March)

Book 3 - Morning Work for Teens with Special Needs Workbook (April, May, June & July)

www.autismclassroom.com

Note: Some images are from Caboose Designs

Made in United States
Orlando, FL
10 January 2025